Lord of the Flies

Classroom Questions

A SCENE BY SCENE TEACHING GUIDE

Amy Farrell

SCENE BY SCENE
ENNISKERRY, IRELAND

Copyright © 2016 by Scene by Scene.

Without limiting the rights under copyright, this book is sold subject to the condition that it shall not, by way of trade or otherwise be lent, resold, hired out, reproduced, stored on or introduced into a retrieval system, or transmitted, in any form or by any means (electronic, mechanical, photocopying, recording or otherwise), or otherwise circulated, without the publisher's prior consent, in any form other than that in which it is published and without a similar condition, including this condition, being imposed on the subsquent publisher.

All rights reserved. No part of this publication may be recorded or transmitted in any form or by any means electronic, mechanical, photocopying, recording or otherwise without the proper consent of the publisher.

The publisher reserves the right to change, without notice, at any time, the specification of this product, whether by change of materials, colours, format, text revision or any other characteristic.

Scene by Scene
Enniskerry
Wicklow, Ireland.
www.scenebysceneguides.com

Lord of the Flies Classroom Questions by Amy Farrell. —1st ed.
ISBN 978-1-910949-48-1

Contents

Chapter 1 - The Sound of the Shell	1
Chapter 2 - Fire on the Mountain	6
Chapter 3 - Huts on the Beach	10
Chapter 4 - Painted Faces and Long Hair	12
Chapter 5 - Beast from Water	18
Chapter 6 - Beast from Air	24
Chapter 7 - Shadows and Tall Trees	27
Chapter 8 - Gift for the Darkness	31
Chapter 9 - A View to a Death	36
Chapter 10 - The Shell and the Glasses	40
Chapter 11 - Castle Rock	44
Chapter 12 - Cry of the Hunters	49
Further Questions	57

Chapter 1
The Sound of the Shell

Summary

As the story begins, two boys struggle through tangled undergrowth after surviving a plane crash.

Ralph leaves the fat boy behind and checks out the shore. He sheds his clothes in the tropical heat, excited by his surroundings.

The fat boy, Piggy, catches up with him, eager to find others and have a meeting.

Ralph blows a conch shell, summoning the other survivors. They arrive in ones and twos, and a group of cloaked boys arrive, marching in line. Their leader, Jack Merridew, had been hoping for grown-ups and a ship and is annoyed to find only other boys.

They tell each other their names and elect Ralph as their chief; he wins more votes than Jack.

Ralph gives Jack control of the boys he came with. They will be the hunters.

Ralph decides to take Jack and Simon with him on an expedition to figure out if they are on an island. Piggy wants to go too, but they don't want him.

The three boys walk along the beach and climb a mountain. From this height they see that they are on an island.

As they return to the others they encounter a piglet tangled in some creepers. Jack takes out his knife, but doesn't strike the animal and it breaks free and runs away. Jack insists that his delay was down to him choosing a place to stab it and declares that he will get it the next time.

Questions

1. What is happening as the chapter begins?

2. What happened to the plane the boys were travelling in?

3. Describe Ralph.

4. Describe the fat boy.

5. Why, do you think, does Ralph leave the fat boy behind and go to the shore?

6. Describe the area around the beach.

7. How do you know that Ralph is happy to be on the beach?

8. How does Ralph treat Piggy?

9. What are your first impressions of Ralph and Piggy?

10. What do the boys do with the conch shell?

11. What does Piggy do as Ralph sounds the conch?

12. Describe the group of boys that assemble under the palm trees.

13. Do you notice anything significant about their clothing?

14. Why is Merridew annoyed when he learns that it was Ralph who summoned the group?

15. What are your first impressions of Merridew?

16. Why does Ralph correct Merridew when he calls Piggy "Fatty"?
What is your response to this?

17. What is the first thing the boys do once they are all assembled?

18. Why does Jack think he should be chief?
Does this tell you anything about his personality?

19. What reasons do the boys have for voting for Ralph?

20. Why, do you think, does Ralph give Jack control of the choir?

21. "There was no lack of boys to choose from."
Why does Ralph choose Simon to accompany him and Jack on their expedition?
Why don't they want Piggy with them, in your opinion?

22. "Now go back, Piggy, and take names."
How does Ralph treat Piggy?

23. Describe the mountain the three boys climb.

24. Do the three boys enjoy their expedition? Explain your answer.

25. What is Ralph's reaction to discovering that they are on an island?
What does this tell you about him?

26. What makes Ralph think that the island is uninhabited?
    Is this clever of him, in your view?

27. What creature do they encounter on the way back down to the others?
    Why does Jack let it get away?
    What would you have done, in his position?

28. How would you feel if you were stranded on an island like these boys are?
    Are they doing well, under the circumstances?
    What problems do you anticipate for them?

Chapter 2
Fire on the Mountain

Summary

Ralph leads another meeting, explaining their situation to the other boys.

Piggy makes the point that nobody knows where they are. Ralph declares that they will have fun until they are rescued.

A small boy asks Ralph about a snake-thing, a "beastie" he saw and is afraid of. Ralph assures him it doesn't exist, but the boys are rattled until Ralph changes the topic by talking of their imminent rescue.

He decides that they will need a fire to signal their presence to passing ships. Full of excitement, the boys head up the mountain.

The boys find deadwood on one side of the mountain and gather it for the fire. Ralph takes Piggy's glasses, despite his protests, and uses them to catch and magnify the sun's rays, as they are without matches.

The woodpile burns, but creates little smoke. As the boys plan how to improve it, Piggy is not allowed to contribute much. He realises that fire has sprung up in the underbrush.

The boys are excited by the fire's destruction. Despite Piggy holding the conch, Jack interrupts him and doesn't let him speak. Piggy points out the problems they are facing and asks where the little kids are. He can't see the boy with a mark on his face, who was afraid of the snake-thing. The boys are frightened when they realise he could be below, in the fire.

Questions

1. Describe the afternoon meeting.

2. Why is Jack eager for the group to establish rules?

3. What point does Piggy make to the group?

4. What does Ralph say they will do until they are rescued?
   Why is he so excited by their predicament?
   Is he behaving naively here, in your view?

5. What does the small boy ask Ralph about?
   How do the boys react to this?

6. What topic does Jack keep returning to?
   Why is this, in your opinion?

7. How does Ralph raise the boys' spirits?

8. What plan of action does he decide on so they will be found?
   Is this a good idea?

9. 'Like a crowd of kids –'
   Why does Piggy think the others are behaving childishly?
   Is he right?

10. Describe Piggy's personality, based on what you have read so far.

11. Describe Ralph's personality, based on what you have read so far.

12. Where do the boys find fuel for the fire?

13. What problem do the boys face once the wood is gathered?
How do they solve this problem?

14. What has helped Ralph and Jack to become friends?

15. 'That was no good.'
Why is Ralph disappointed with the fire?

16. What does Jack volunteer to do for the group?

17. How is Piggy treated by the others?
Why do they treat him this way, in your opinion?

18. What have the boys accidentally done?

19. How do the boys react to the outbreak of fire?
What is your response to this?

20. What different problems does Piggy highlight for the group?

21. What is the mood like as the chapter ends? Explain your view.

Chapter 3
Huts on the Beach

Summary

The chapter begins with Jack hunting unsuccessfully in the forest.

Time has passed since the boys' arrival on the island.

Ralph and the other boys are building a shelter, but Ralph complains that the others keep running off and so it will never be done.

Ralph and Jack argue over the need for shelters and Jack's hunting. They agree that they need some kind of a home for the little ones.

Jack is obsessed with the idea of catching and killing a pig and talks of little else.

Simon goes into the forest alone, unnoticed by Ralph and Jack. He finds a secluded spot for himself as night falls.

Questions

1. What is Jack doing as the chapter begins?
   Do you think he knows what he is doing? Explain your view.

2. What problems do they face, building the shelters?

3. What do Ralph and Jack argue about?
   Which of the boys do you agree with? Explain your view.

4. What feeling does Jack admit to having while hunting?

5. Where does Simon go while Jack and Ralph are talking?
   Why does he do this, do you think?

6. Are the boys coping well with their circumstances in your view? Explain your answer.

7. Is Ralph a good leader?

Chapter 4
Painted Faces and Long Hair

Summary

The author describes life on the island. For the 'littluns' there is fruit-eating, stomach-ache, fear at night and play.

Roger, one of the older boys, throws stones at Henry, a 'littlun,' down by the lagoon's edge. He throws the stones near, but not at, the other boy.

Roger is interrupted by Jack's arrival. Jack smears himself in clay to camouflage himself while hunting. He is delighted with the effect of the red and white and black on his face. The hunters go in pursuit of pigs.

Piggy suggests making a sundial to Ralph, but Ralph doesn't listen to him. Piggy is an outsider, isolated by the group.

Ralph spots smoke from a ship's funnel out at sea. Realising their fire on the mountain is out, Ralph takes off through the undergrowth, followed by Simon and Maurice.

Their fire has burnt out and the ship passes them by.

Ralph blames the hunters for letting the fire go out. They watch as the hunters return, carrying the dead carcass of a pig.

Jack is thrilled with their kill, but all Ralph speaks about is the fact that they let the fire go out. He tells them about the ship passing by.

Piggy tells Jack he shouldn't have let the fire go out and Jack punches him in the stomach. Piggy's glasses are broken.

Jack apologises about the fire. They cook and share the meat. Jack doesn't want to share with Piggy, as he didn't participate in the hunt.

Ralph calls a meeting.

Questions

1. What is daily life like on the island?

2. Describe Percival.
   Do you feel sorry for him?

3. What is life on the island like for the 'littluns'?

4. What does Roger do to Henry?
   What is your reaction to this?
   Do you think he is likely to do something like this again?

5. What do Roger's actions tell you about 'society' on the island?

6. What does Jack need the clay for?

7. Is Jack happy with his "mask"?

8. What idea does Piggy approach Ralph with by the bathing-pool?
   Do you think it is a good idea?

9. Do Ralph and the other boys like Piggy?
   What is your reaction to this?

10. What does Ralph spot out at sea?

11. What do the boys realise about their fire on the mountain?

12. Describe the atmosphere at this point.

13. Why is Ralph "agonized by indecision" as he climbs the slope?
    What would you do in his position?

14. What state is the fire in when Ralph reaches it?
    How would you feel, in his position?

15. How does Ralph react to the ship passing them by?

16. Describe the hunters' procession.

17. "Simon looked now, from Ralph to Jack, as he had looked from Ralph to the horizon, and what he saw seemed to make him afraid."
    What is going on here, do you think?

18. What do the hunters chant?
    What is your reaction to their words here?

19. Is Ralph impressed by their bounty?

20. Do you feel sorry for Jack here?

21. What reasons does Ralph have for being annoyed with Jack?

22. Why does Jack strike Piggy?
    What is your reaction to this?

23. Why do the boys treat Piggy so poorly?

24. Do they underestimate Piggy, in your view?

25. What effect does Jack's apology have on the group?

26. How do they light the fire?

27. "Not even Ralph knew how a link between him and Jack had been snapped and fastened elsewhere."
What is going on here?
Does this changing allegiance surprise you?

28. 'You didn't hunt.'
How does Simon respond when Jack doesn't give Piggy any meat?
What does this suggest about Simon's character?

29. What does Maurice do to bring the boys together again?

30. How well are the boys getting on?

31. Do you think killing the pig was a necessary or savage act? Explain your view.

32. How could the killing of the pig upset or affect the 'society' on the island?

33. Do you feel apprehensive about what will happen next? What makes you feel this way?

34. Describe the atmosphere as the chapter ends.

35. How are things changing between the boys?
What is bringing about these changes?

36. What different sections of society could the different boys represent? Explain your answer.

Chapter 5
Beast from Water

Summary

Ralph, in reflective mood, prepares for a serious assembly with the boys. He brings up each of the tasks they agreed upon and left undone and stresses the importance of their signal fire.

When Jack speaks he accuses the littluns of being crybabies and sissies for being afraid. He insists that there is no beast on the island.

Piggy says they must get the littluns to speak, to show them how silly their fears are. Phil speaks of nightmares and a figure in the forest that turns out to be Simon. Percival, after much crying, tells Jack that the beast comes out of the sea. This notion rattles the boys.

The meeting deteriorates into a discussion about ghosts as darkness falls. Ralph feels that the meeting has broken down.

Jack shouts out against Ralph and the rules, saying he'll hunt down any beast there is and the assembly disintegrates.

Ralph doesn't sound the conch to call the boys back for fear they won't obey him. He wants to give up being chief, but Piggy is adamant that he continue. He fears that Jack would hurt him if Ralph were not chief.

Questions

1. "He lost himself in a maze of thoughts that were rendered vague by his lack of words to express them."
   Why does Ralph find it difficult to express himself?
   Is his age a factor here?

2. "This meeting must not be fun, but business."
   Why does Ralph want the meeting to be serious?
   Is he a good leader for the boys, in your view?

3. What makes Ralph begin to realise Piggy's worth as this chapter begins?

4. Why does Piggy stand outside the triangle?
   Do you understand why he feels this way?

5. What tasks have the boys neglected to do?
   Is Ralph right to be frustrated and annoyed by this or is he being too uptight and serious in your view?

6. What is hygiene like on the island?
   What is your reaction to this?

7. 'Can't you see we ought to - ought to die before we let the fire out?'
   Is the fire really this important?

8. How do the boys react to Ralph's speech and his rule about lighting cooking fires?

9.   'You voted me for chief. Now you do what I say.'
Do you think the others will obey Ralph? Explain your view.

10.   'Anyway, you don't hunt or build or help - you're a lot of cry-babies and sissies.'
Is Jack fair in what he says of the littluns?

11.   '...but there is no beast in the forest.'
Do you think the boys are reassured by Jack's words?
How do you expect them to respond to the mention of a beast?

12.   Does Piggy believe in a beast?
What does he think they might fear in future?
What is your reaction to this idea?
How do the boys react?
Why do they react this way?

13.   What was Phil's nightmare about?
Does it sound frightening to you?
What makes it frightening for the other boys?

14.   "No-one had seen the mulberry-coloured birthmark again."
What is significant about this boy's disappearance?
Why does nobody mention his disappearance now?

15.   Why, do you think, does Percival start crying?
What makes the other littluns join in?

16. Are the littluns being cared for on the island?
    Should the older boys be responsible for them?

17. What makes the littluns stop crying?

18. 'He says the beast comes out of the sea.'
    How do the boys react to Percival's statement about the beast?
    How would you feel, in their position?

19. How does Maurice add to the discussion of the beast?

20. What does Simon try to tell the others?
    Why does he fail to make his point?
    Is he right to some extent, do you think?

21. "The world, that understandable and lawful world, was slipping away."
    What makes Ralph feel that things are breaking down?

22. 'What's grown-ups going to think?'
    Is Piggy justified in feeling so annoyed with the group?

23. 'Bollocks to the rules!'
    What has made Jack react like this?
    Whose side are you on, Ralph's or Jack's? Explain your allegiance.

24. 'We'll be like animals. We'll never be rescued.'
    Do you think the boys are behaving like animals?
    Why aren't rules and order working?
    What, if anything, could they do differently to maintain order on the island?

25. Why does Ralph want to give up being chief?

26. Why does Piggy insist that Ralph cannot give up?

27. Do you think Jack would hurt Piggy, given the chance?
    Do you think Ralph can protect Piggy from Jack?

28. 'At home there was always a grown-up.'
    Comment on this line.

29. What is the atmosphere like as the chapter ends?

30. How is life on the island changing?

31. Are the boys themselves changing and adjusting?
    Use examples to support your point of view.

Chapter 6
Beast from Air

Summary

While the boys sleep, there is an explosion overhead and a figure parachutes down to the island.

The twins, tending the fire, are terrified when they see this figure and they go straight to Ralph.

Once day breaks the boys have a meeting. Jack is eager to hunt the beast. Ralph is concerned with looking after the littluns.

The boys leave an ailing Piggy behind to look after the younger boys as they go in search of the beast.

Their search takes them down to the sea. Once again, Ralph is annoyed when the others explore and play, rather than focusing on their smoke signal. Despite their protests, Ralph insists that they all head towards their fire on the mountain.

Questions

1. What "sign" is there in the sky from the "world of grown-ups"?

2. What happens the figure as he falls from the sky?

3. "...the figure sat on the mountain-top and bowed and sank and bowed again."
   Why does the figure move like this?

4. What frightens the twins as they tend the fire?

5. How do the boys describe the beast to the assembly?

6. "Johnny, yawning still, burst into noisy tears and was slapped by Bill till he choked on them."
   Comment on this.

7. What different attitudes do the boys have towards caring for the littluns?

8. Can you compare the littluns to any section of our society?

9. What is wrong with Piggy as the boys decide what to do next?
   Are you surprised that nobody checks on him?

10. What do Simon's and Ralph's thoughts as they go in search of the beast tell you about their personalities?
    Are the boys under a lot of pressure, do you think?

11. What makes Ralph go out onto the neck of land?

12. How does the author describe the Pacific?
    How does this add to the atmosphere?

13. What major differences do you see between Jack and Ralph in this chapter?

14. Describe Simon's character.

15. Why is Ralph frustrated by the other boys time and again?
    Is he too hard on them, do you think?

16. Does Ralph have good control of the boys?
    Is he a good leader, in your view?
    Is he a better leader than Jack would be?

Chapter 7
Shadows and Tall Trees

Summary

Ralph notes how scruffy he and his companions have become as they stop to eat fruit. Gazing out to sea, Ralph feels that rescue is impossible, but Simon assures him that he'll return home.

Steaming pig droppings are sighted and Jack takes up the hunt. They startle a boar and Ralph wounds him with his spear, but the animal escapes.

Re-living and joking about the incident, the boys begin to 'hunt' Robert, but get carried away. They jab him and chant about killing him, hurting and frightening him with their game.

Despite some reluctance, the boys make their way by the sea towards the mountain. The going is slow and difficult.

Ralph is anxious not to leave Piggy alone all night with the littluns, so Simon volunteers to cross the island to tell him they'll be back after dark.

Jack jibes at Ralph and Ralph asks Jack why he hates him, but gets no answer.

When they reach the mountain, darkness has fallen and the boys are afraid to venture up it. Jack insists on going and Ralph accepts his offer to accompany him. The only other boy to go is Roger.

Ralph realises how foolish this venture is and stops, but Jack defiantly carries on alone.

When he comes back Jack tells Ralph and Roger that he saw a thing on top of the mountain. Ralph says that they'll go and look.

Ralph is scared, but approaches the thing that looks something like an ape, before the three boys flee.

Questions

1. What does Ralph dislike about his appearance?

2. Describe the sea on this side of the island.

3. How does Simon make Ralph feel a bit better as he looks out to sea?
   Do you think Simon is right?

4. Describe the house on the edge of the moors that Ralph and his family lived in.
   What is the effect of this memory in the story?

5. What does Ralph's choice of books in this memory tell you about him?

6. What does Ralph do when the boar charges?

7. What do the boys do to Robert?
   What is your reaction to their behaviour here?
   What has led to this?

8. What is your reaction to Jack's joke about hunting a littlun?

9. What does Simon volunteer to do to help Ralph?
   Is this brave of him?

10. 'Why do you hate me?'
    Why does Jack hate Ralph, in your view?

11. 'I'm going up the mountain.'
    Night is falling and the boys are tired. What makes Jack want to go up the mountain, in your opinion?

12. Would you accompany Ralph and Jack if you were there? Give reasons for your answer.

13. 'We're being fools.'
    Why does Ralph stop going upwards?
    Is this the smart thing to do?
    What makes Jack continue on?
    What is your reaction to this?

14. What does Jack say he has seen on the mountain-top?
    How does Ralph react to this information?

15. Is Ralph scared when they reach the top?

16. Describe the atmosphere at this point.

17. What does the moonlight reveal?

18. Why do the boys run away?

Chapter 8
Gift for the Darkness

Summary

Ralph doesn't know what to do about the beast on the mountain-top, he thinks the boys are no match for it, something that insults Jack.

Jack calls an assembly and declares that Ralph isn't a proper chief, calling him a coward. He asks the boys to vote against Ralph being their chief, but they don't do so. Jack goes off by himself, no longer wanting to be part of Ralph's group.

Piggy suggests building a fire down where they are, overcoming the problem of the beast on the mountain. The boys work together to build a fire on the sand by the platform. Ralph realises that a lot of the bigger boys have left.

Jack plans to kill a pig and have a feast to get more boys onside. He and his hunters find a sow with piglets that they wound and chase. She finally collapses in a clearing and they brutally stab her while Jack cuts her throat.

They cut off her head and leave it on a spike, as a gift for the beast.

Later, Simon comes across the pig's head and the flies that circle it.

Ralph and Piggy are concerned about fetching enough wood to keep the fire going.

Jack and some hunters come to steal fire from Piggy and Ralph's group. Jack invites the others to come and see his tribe.

When the hunters leave, the others have a meeting where Ralph stresses the importance of the fire for rescue.

Simon has an imaginary conversation with the Lord of the Flies. It speaks menacingly to him, before he falls unconscious.

Questions

1. How does Ralph describe the beast?

2. Why can't they have a signal fire?

3. How does Ralph offend Jack?

4. 'He isn't a proper chief.'
   What stops the boys from voting against Ralph, in your opinion?

5. What makes Jack go off by himself?
   Is this a childish thing to do, in your view?

6. What is your view of Jack's character at this point?

7. How does Piggy solve the problem of the beast guarding their fire on the mountain?

8. Where have the missing bigger boys gone to?
   Would you have gone too, in their position? Explain your decision.

9. What do Jack's group decide to do about the beast?

10. Why does Jack intend to kill a pig?
    Is this a good strategy?

11. Describe the pigs the boys find.

12. "...the sow staggered her way ahead of them, bleeding and mad, and the hunters followed..."
    What is your reaction to the way the boys hunt the sow?
    Do they sound cruel to you?
    Comment on the injuries they inflict on the animal.
    Does anything stand out? Explain your answer.

13. Why do the hunters leave the pig's head behind?
    What does this suggest about what they believe?

14. How does Simon react to the sight of the pig's spiked head?

15. Why does he think of the pig head as the "Lord of the Flies"?
    Comment on this image.

16. Why are Ralph and Piggy worried about the fire?

17. Describe the appearance of the boys who come to steal fire.

18. Do you feel sorry for Ralph and his group here?

19. What message does Jack have for the remaining boys?

20. Jack refers to his "tribe". Does this tell you anything about the state of affairs on the island?

21. How does the approaching storm contribute to the atmosphere?

22. What does Simon's imagined conversation with the Lord of the Flies reveal to you about him?
    How does this scene add to the atmosphere and storyline?

23. What happens Simon as the chapter ends?

24. What, do you think, will happen next?
    Why do you think this?

Chapter 9
A View to a Death

Summary

A storm is brewing.

Simon suffers a nosebleed and seizure, alone beside the pig's head, the Lord of the Flies. He comes to and walks through the forest. He finds himself out in the open and discovers the parachute and human remains. He spies smoke and decides to find the others to tell them the truth about the beast.

Ralph, Piggy and some littluns are the only ones by the bathing pool. The others have gone to join Jack. Piggy suggests that they should go too.

They hear Jack's party before they arrive. The boys fall silent as they approach. Jack invites them to take some meat. Jack tells the boys to sit down and asks who will join his tribe.

Ralph points out that he was elected chief, but boys agree to join Jack's tribe. A thunderstorm breaks and Piggy tells Ralph to come away before trouble starts.

As the lightning flashes, Jack and the boys begin to dance and chant, *'Kill the beast! Cut his throat! Spill his blood!'*

Simon emerges from the forest, telling of the dead man on the hill. The crowd surge forward after him, screaming and striking him.

Rain pours down and the crowd breaks up, revealing a small, bloody body.

Wind catches the parachute of the dead man on the hill and blows the figure down past the lagoon and out to sea.

After midnight, the storm passes and the tide carries Simon's dead body away.

Questions

1. What is happening to Simon as this chapter begins?

2. What does Simon discover out in the open on the rock?
   Is Simon brave here?
   How does Simon react to his discovery?

3. Despite his weakness, Simon heads towards camp to tell the others the truth about the beast straight away. What does this tell you about his character?

4. Why are there so few boys at the bathing pool?
   Would you stay with Ralph, or go with Jack, if you were on the island?

5. What reason does Piggy give for wanting to join Jack and the others?

6. Describe Jack's party.

7. How do the boys react when they see Ralph and Piggy?

8. How does Jack react to Ralph and Piggy's arrival?

9. How does Jack act to show he's in charge?
   What different things does he do to demonstrate his authority?

10. What is significant about Jack's mask?

11. How does the thunderstorm contribute to the atmosphere here?

12. '...the conch doesn't count at this end of the island-'
    Do you think Jack has successfully taken control of the island?
    How serious is this development?

13. Comment on the imagery as the boys dance chanting in the thunderstorm.

14. What happens when Simon emerges from the forest?
    Why does this happen?
    What is your reaction to this?

15. What happens to the dead body on the hill?

16. "Towards midnight the rain ceased and the clouds drifted away..."
    Comment on the imagery in the closing section of this chapter.

17. "...Simon's dead body moved out towards the open sea."
    What is your reaction to this development?
    How do you feel as the chapter ends?

18. How do you expect Simon's death to impact on the boys of the island?

Chapter 10
The Shell and the Glasses

Summary

Ralph is injured and limping when he joins Piggy on the platform. Ralph says that Simon was murdered, but Piggy doesn't want to talk about it, saying that the group had been scared and anything might have happened.

Ralph says that he's frightened of the boys, of themselves, and wants to go home.

Piggy says they shouldn't tell Samneric that they were in the dance, saying that they were on the outside. Ralph agrees to this version of the story.

When they see Sam and Eric, the twins are also sporting injuries. They claim to have left the party early, as do Piggy and Ralph. They all know what they participated in, but no-one speaks of it.

Roger is challenged as he approaches Castle Rock. He says that the Chief has decided to beat Wilfred and has tied him up.

When he reaches the tribe they are lying in a semi-circle before the Chief.

Wilfred, freshly beaten and sniffing, is in the background.

The Chief declares that the next day some of them will hunt, while others will stay behind to improve the cave and defend the gate from the others and the beast.

Maurice and Roger will go with the Chief to steal fire from the others.

Ralph, Piggy and Samneric are having difficulties keeping their fire going. They decide to let it out at night and go to the first shelter.

They hear noises outside and a voice whispers that it has come for Piggy.

Piggy has an asthma attack and a brawl breaks out in the shelter, before the hunters run away. In the confusion, Ralph and Eric fight with one another, not the attacking hunters.

The Chief and his accomplices return to Castle Rock with Piggy's glasses.

Questions

1. What condition is Ralph in as the chapter begins?

2. How does Piggy react when Ralph mentions Simon's murder?
   Why does he react like this, in your view?

3. What different excuses does Piggy come up with for what they did to Simon?

4. "There was loathing, and at the same time a kind of feverish excitement in his voice."
   Explain Ralph's mixed emotions here.

5. 'I'm frightened. Of us.'
   Explain what Ralph means here.

6. What version of events do Ralph and Piggy decide to tell Samneric?
   What is significant about this?

7. Did Sam and Eric really leave the party early?
   How do you know?

8. What is significant about the boys' injuries?
   What does it tell you about the attack on Simon?
   How do you expect this to affect them?

9. What has happened to Wilfred?
   Why has this happened?
   What is your response to this?

10. What does Jack tell the tribe, to create the sense that their camp needs to be defended?
    Does anything he says here surprise you?

11. How does the Chief intend to get fire?

12. 'We don't want another night without fire.'
    Why is having a fire so important to the boys?

13. What reason does Piggy have for not helping to gather firewood?

14. 'If we don't go home soon we'll be barmy.'
    Is Piggy right to be so concerned? Explain your view.

15. What do Ralph's group hear outside the shelter?
    How do they react?

16. 'That was Jack and his hunters…Why can't they leave us alone?'
    Can you answer Ralph's question?

17. Did Ralph's group defend themselves successfully?

18. What did the hunters come for?
    What is your reaction to this development?

Chapter 11
Castle Rock

Summary

The four boys try to bring their fire alight, to no avail. Ralph blows the conch and some littluns join them.

Piggy wants his glasses and Ralph continues to insist on the need for a fire. They decide to approach Jack's group. Piggy wants to tell Jack to return his glasses because it is the 'right' thing to do.

They eat and prepare to face the others. The boys walk along the beach to Castle Rock. When they arrive, Ralph blows the conch. Roger throws a stone between the twins.

Jack and two hunters arrive with a dead, headless sow. Jack tells Ralph to go back to his end of the island. Ralph tells him to return Piggy's glasses and calls him a thief, so Jack rushes at him with his spear and the boys fight.

Ralph addresses the group of savages, accusing them of not playing the game. He says that they must return Piggy's glasses and keep a signal fire going.

Jack orders the boys to grab the twins and tie them up, which they do. Ralph loses his temper and charges at Jack and the pair fight fiercely.

Piggy asks to speak and the tribe boo him. He accuses them of acting like little kids and pretending to be savages. He asks whether chaos or order is better, while all the time Roger throws down stones from above.

The boys of the tribe shout and prepare to charge, when Roger levers free the giant boulder. It strikes Piggy a glancing blow and smashes the conch. Piggy is flung onto the red rock in the sea and bangs his head. His arms and legs twitch and his body is washed out to sea.

Jack screams that there's no tribe for Ralph anymore, that the conch is gone. He hurls his spear at Ralph, hitting him. The tribe advance on Ralph, throwing spears, and he runs away into the forest.

The Chief tells Samneric they have to join the tribe and pokes Sam in the ribs, before Roger advances on them.

Questions

1. What do the four remaining boys in Ralph's group decide to do next?
   What would you do, in their position?

2. Is Piggy's decision to confront Jack a brave move?
   Is it a wise move, in your view?

3. Is Piggy badly off without his glasses?

4. 'But they'll be painted! You know how it is-'
   What is the significance of the face painting?

5. 'I knew all the time. I hadn't forgotten.'
   Does Ralph often lose his train of thought?
   Has this affected his ability to lead the boys, in your view?

6. Why have so many boys chosen to join Jack's tribe, in your view?
   Is this a realistic aspect of the novel?

7. How do Jack's tribe react when they see the other boys?
   Describe the atmosphere at this point.
   What, do you think, will happen next?

8. Ralph blows the conch as he approaches Castle Rock.
   Is this a good strategy, in your view?

9. 'Ralph! Don't leave me!'
   Why is Piggy so scared as Jack arrives?
   Do you feel sorry for him here?

10. "Jack made a rush and stabbed at Ralph's chest with his spear."
    What made Jack attack Ralph?
    Does this surprise you?

11. Ralph accuses Jack's tribe of not "playing the game".
    Is this all a game, in your opinion?

12. "They felled the twins clumsily and excitedly."
    Is Jack a powerful leader?
    Why do the boys obey him?

13. Describe the fight between Jack and Ralph.

14. How do the boys react to Piggy's request to speak?
    Why do they react like this?

15. How does Piggy describe their behaviour?
    Is he accurate in what he says about them?

16. Describe the scene as Jack's tribe prepare to charge.
    Is this a cinematic moment? Explain.

17. What weapon does Roger release?
    Are you surprised by this development?

18. What damage does the great rock do?

19. How is Piggy's death described?
    What is your reaction to this event?

20. Have matters on the island got out of hand?
    Should order be restored?
    Can order be restored in your view?

21. What does Jack do immediately after Piggy's death?
    What is your reaction to this?

22. Are you surprised when the boys of the tribe throw their spears at Ralph?
    Why do they do this?

23. What is the atmosphere like as the chapter ends?

24. What do you expect to happen to Sam and Eric?

25. Is Roger a dangerous or threatening character? Explain your view.

26. Roger is described as "one wielding a nameless authority." What does this expression mean?
    Do his actions in this chapter concern you?

27. Is it significant that the conch was smashed as Piggy died? Is there a deeper meaning to these two events happening at the same time?

Chapter 12
Cry of the Hunters

Summary

Ralph lies in a covert, wondering about the extent of his injuries, listening out for the others who seem reluctant to enter the darkness of the forest.

In the late afternoon Ralph goes to see what the tribe are doing and realises they are cooking the pig.

After returning to the platform, Ralph decides to try Jack's group again, hoping for more success now that they have eaten.

He comes across the pig skull in a forest clearing and lashes out at it.

When night falls, Ralph approaches Castle Rock and sees that there is still an armed watchman on look-out duty.

He hears the chant and knows the tribe are dancing.

He is disheartened when he recognises Simon and Eric on guard duty. Ralph climbs up the rock to them. Sam tries to send him away. They tell him to leave, saying that the Chief and Roger intend to hunt and kill him the following day. The boys have been told that the hunt will be dangerous, and that they should throw their spears, like at a pig. They plan to search the island from end to end for him.

Ralph insists that he hasn't done anything, except want to keep a fire going. He realises that the hunters intend to do him serious harm, something that the twins attribute to Roger and the Chief.

Someone approaches, so Ralph quickly explains that he will hide nearby in a thicket during the hunt. He leaves with a chunk of meat that Sam gives him.

Ralph settles down for the night, after hearing cries of pain and anger coming from the look-out tower.

The next morning he wakes to hear the boys calling to one another, sweeping the island for him. He worms his way into the thicket and discovers that the giant rock that killed Piggy created a hollow in it when it bounced.

He waits to hear the boys moving off, but instead hears Jack questioning the twins about whether or not this is the right thicket.

Ralph knows that it would take a week for them to break through the thicket and plans to use his spear against anyone who worms their way through.

The tribe bounce a huge boulder down through the thicket, smashing it, and then heave another. Ralph is thrown into the air with the impact.

A spear appears through the branches. Ralph panics and jabs his own spear through, hitting someone. Someone moans, while another voice says that

Ralph is dangerous.

They set the thicket on fire and Ralph retreats towards the forest. He stabs a savage in his path and runs through the undergrowth.

Ralph considers climbing a tree or bursting through their lines, but feels these are terrible options to choose from. He thinks about hiding.

Hearing a cry, he runs again, back into the clearing with the pig skull and realises that the others have set the island on fire.

He decides that hiding gives him the best chance and looks around as he runs, choosing a space about a foot high, covered in by bushes and tangled creepers. The fire sweeps the island, Ralph hears it and the cries of the boys.

A savage carrying a spear approaches Ralph's hiding place. He utters his cry and Ralph notices that his spear is sharpened at both ends. Ralph stays quiet.

The savage peers into the thicket and Ralph screams and bursts out into the thicket, running away again.

He has to swerve to avoid the flames as the boys call out, all running now. Ralph runs to the beach, where he meets a naval officer.

The officer sees a ragged group of boys playing war and asks if there's any adults or dead on the island. He believes Ralph when he says two were killed.

The officer is disappointed to hear they don't know how many of them there are. Ralph says he's the boss when they are asked who is in charge.

Ralph begins to weep, as do the little boys.

Questions

1. Describe Ralph's injuries.

2. "This was a savage whose image refused to blend with that ancient picture of a boy in shorts and shirt."
   Has their time on the island transformed the boys into savages? Explain your view.

3. "These painted savages would go further and further."
   Is Ralph right here, in expecting the tribe's behaviour to worsen? Explain your view.

4. What makes Ralph decide to return to the tribe again?

5. What does Ralph do when he finds the pigskull?
   Can you explain his reaction here?

6. Why is Ralph afraid to sleep?
   What would you do, in his position?

7. "...he knew he was an outcast."
   Do you feel sorry for Ralph?
   Give reasons for your answer.

8. What has become of Samneric?

9. How do Sam and Eric react to seeing Ralph?
   Does this surprise you?

10. What are the Chief and Roger planning to do the following day?
    What is your reaction to this?

11. What instructions have the boys been given for the hunt?
    What is going on here?
    How would you feel if you were Ralph?

12. Is Ralph being treated fairly by the others?
    Why are they so much against him?

13. What will happen to Ralph if the hunt for him is successful?

14. Where does Ralph plan to hide the next day?
    Is this a good strategy, in your view?

15. 'Roger sharpened a stick at both ends.'
    What does Roger intend to do to Ralph when he catches him?
    What is your reaction to this?
    Are you surprised by Roger here? Justify your view.

16. Where does Ralph decide to sleep for the night?
    What is his reasoning behind this?

17. What does Ralph hear while he eats?
    What is going on, do you think?

18. Are you surprised that Ralph stays so close to Castle Rock?
    Do you feel sorry for him at this point?

19. What stroke of luck does Ralph have with his hiding place?

20. What made the twins lead the others to the thicket?
    Do you judge them harshly for their actions here?

21. Is Ralph worried about the tribe breaking a path through the thicket to find him?

22. How do Jack's tribe 'search' the thicket?
    What is your reaction to their actions here?

23. How does Ralph react when a spear is thrust through the thicket?
    Do you understand his reaction?

24. 'See? I told you - he's dangerous.'
    Is Ralph dangerous?
    What has made him this way?
    What does this suggest about violence?

25. How do they flush Ralph out of the thicket?
    Is this a clever idea?

26. "Ralph launched himself like a cat; stabbed, snarling, with the spear, and the savage doubled up."
    Do you condone or condemn Ralph's actions here?
    Are the boys still 'playing'?

27. What are Ralph's escape options, as he sees them?

28. Why does he decide that hiding is the best option?
    Do you agree with him?

29. Where does Ralph hide?

30. What does Ralph do when he's spotted?

31. "He shot forward, burst the thicket, was in the open screaming, snarling, bloody."
    Comment on this image.

32. Who does Ralph discover on the beach?
    What is your reaction to this?
    What does this mean for Ralph?
    What does it mean for the others?

33. How do the boys appear in the officer's eyes?

34. What makes the officer disappointed in the boys?

35. Why does Ralph give in to tears *now*?
    What does he cry about?

36. Percival Wemys Madison can't remember his name.
    What is your reaction to this?

37. How did the naval officers find them?
    Is this ironic?

38. Did the officers arrive just in time for Ralph?

39. What would have happened, in your opinion, if the navy hadn't arrived at this moment?

40. How have the boys changed during their time on the island?
Do you think they will return to life as normal now? Explain your view.

Further Questions

1. What does this novel suggest about human nature?

2. What does this novel suggest about violence and rules?

3. Do you think something like the events in this novel could really happen? Explain your view.

4. Who was your favourite character?
   What did you like about them?

5. Which character did you dislike most?
   What did you dislike about them?

6. How does the author's use of imagery and description add to this story?

7. What different things does fire symbolise in this novel?

8. How does the author make use of foreshadowing to add to the story?

9. How does the author make use of tension to add to the story?

10. How does the author make use of atmosphere to add to the story?

11. What was your favourite section of the story?
    Why did this part appeal to you?

12. What was the saddest section of the story?
    What made it moving and sad?

13. What did you like about this novel? Give examples in your answer.

14. What did you dislike about this novel? Give examples in your answer.

15. Does this novel remind you of any other novels or films? Explain your view.

CLASSROOM QUESTIONS GUIDES

Books of questions, designed to save teachers time and lead to rewarding classroom experiences.

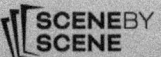

www.SceneBySceneGuides.com

www.ingramcontent.com/pod-product-compliance
Lightning Source LLC
Chambersburg PA
CBHW071035080526
44587CB00015B/2622